DIVORCE is a Piece of Cake

Inspirational Cookbook on surviving divorce

by

Eric Richard Williams

authorHOUSE

1663 LIBERTY DRIVE, SUITE 200
BLOOMINGTON, INDIANA 47403
(800) 839-8640
www.authorhouse.com

© 2004 Eric Richard Williams
All Rights Reserved.

No part of this book may be reproduced, stored in a retrieval system, or transmitted by any means without the written permission of the author.

First published by AuthorHouse 07/06/04

ISBN: 1-4184-3482-5 (e)
ISBN: 1-4184-3483-3 (sc)

Printed in the United States of America
Bloomington, Indiana

This book is printed on acid-free paper.

Dedication

To my wonderful family

Karen Williams
Merlene Williams
Jerry Williams
Andre Williams
Sharlene Williams
Tonya Mullen
Eric Mullen

Special thanks to

SUSAN MARIE FISHER

For all of your outstanding

help and support,

I could not have done it without you.

Wedding Cake on Cover

Provided By

A PIECE OF CAKE BAKERY
3537 Kifer Road
Santa Clara, CA 95051
(408) 524-8180

MENU

GOD'S RECIPES 1

DIVORCE COURT CAKE 3
LONELINESS CAKE 4
FEAR CAKE 5
SUICIDE CAKE 6
POSITIVE ATTITUDE CAKE 7
MOTIVATION CAKE 8
HEALING CAKE 9
PROTECTION CAKE 10
LOVE CAKE 11
STRENGTH CAKE 12
ENEMY CAKE 13
RAISING YOUR CHILD CAKE 14
CHEATED ON CAKE 15
REJECTION CAKE 16
BANKRUPTCY CAKE 17
OVERCOMER CAKE 18
DEPRESSION CAKE 19
CRISIS CAKE 20
BROKEN HEART CAKE 21
PEACE CAKE 22
PATIENCE CAKE 23
JOY CAKE 24
FALSE ACCUSATION CAKE 25
ENCOURAGEMENT CAKE 26
FAITH CAKE 27
ANGER CAKE 28
HELP CAKE 29

MENU

    GOOD CAKE 30
    DATING AGAIN CAKE 31
    RE-MARRIAGE CAKE 32

INSPIRATIONAL SLICES................................... 33

THE BAKERY 81

    STRAWBERRY "SHORT" CAKE
        SHORT TERM GOALS.. 83

    CHOCOLATE "DREAM" CAKE
        LONG TERM DREAMS 84

    BIRTHDAY CAKE
        HOW I WILL CELEBRATE MY NEXT BIRTHDAY 85

    FUN-NEL CAKE
        FUN THINGS I LIKE TO DO... 86

    CRAB CAKE
        THINGS THAT MAKE ME ANGRY 87

    ANGEL FOOD CAKE
        SPECIAL PEOPLE GOD PLACED IN MY LIFE 88

    ICE CREAM CAKE
        PEOPLE I NEED TO FORGIVE AND STOP GIVING THE "COLD" SHOULDER 89

    POUND CAKE
        MY WEIGHT LOSS GOALS 90

    FRUIT CAKE
        POOR DECISIONS I MADE IN THE PAST 91

    PANCAKE
        THINGS I NEED TO THANK GOD FOR EVERY MORNING 92

    CRUMB CAKE
        BIBLE SCRIPTURES THAT KEPT ME FROM CRUMBLING 93

    GOURMET CAKE
        NICE THINGS I DESIRE TO HAVE IN LIFE 94

MENU

SPONGE CAKE
    NEGATIVE PEOPLE WHO SOAK UP ALL OF MY ENERGY 95

CHEESECAKE
    THINKING ABOUT THESE THINGS MAKES ME SMILE 96

NUT CAKE
    TYPES OF BEHAVIOR I WILL NOT TOLERATE IN MY NEXT RELATIONSHIP 97

DEVILS FOOD CAKE
    AREAS OF PERSONAL WEAKNESS 98

COFFEE CAKE
    REASONS WHY I DESERVE A BREAK 99

UPSIDE DOWN CAKE
    HOW WILL I TURN MY LIFE AROUND 100

ICING ON THE CAKE
    THINGS I LOVE ABOUT MYSELF 101

TASTY CAKE
    THINGS I CAN DO TO MAKE MY "BITTER" SITUATION "TASTE" BETTER 102

CAKE MIX
    PLACES I CAN GO TO "MIX" WITH NEW PEOPLE 103

RICE CAKE
    THINGS I CAN DO TO "LIGHTEN" MY CHILDREN'S LOAD 104

FISH CAKE
    REASONS WHY I MUST KEEP "SWIMMING" AND NOT ALLOW DIVORCE TO CAUSE ME TO "SINK" 105

CAKE CANDLES
    PEOPLE WHO SUPPORTED ME WHEN THINGS WERE "DARK" 106

MENU

BAKE SALE
MY FINANCIAL GOALS 107

CUP CAKE
SMALL THINGS I CAN DO TO HELP OTHERS 108

"CARAT" CAKE
WHAT IS THE CURRENT VALUE OF MY WEDDING RINGS AND WHAT I PLAN TO DO WITH THEM 109

HOMEMADE CAKE
WHAT IS THE CURRENT VALUE OF MY HOME AND WHAT I PLAN TO DO WITH IT 110

BEEF CAKE
"BEEFS" I NEED TO RESOLVE WITH MY "X" IN A PEACEFUL MANNER 111

WEDDING CAKE
TYPE OF WEDDING I DESIRE WHEN I REMARRY 112

BANANA CAKE
REASONS I SHOULD STOP "MONKEYING" AROUND AND MOVE ON WITH MY LIFE 113

WHIPPED CREAM
THINGS I CAN DO TO STAY ON "TOP" OF MY EMOTIONS 114

NAPKINS
NEGATIVE WORDS I NEED TO "WIPE" OUT OF MY MOUTH 115

CAKE JOURNAL **117**

*All Scripture quotations are taken from the King James Version of the Bible and The New Century Version of the Bible.

GOD'S RECIPES

GOD'S RECIPE...
DIVORCE COURT CAKE

3 CUPS FLOUR
> ISAIAH 26:3 **THOU WILT KEEP HIM IN PERFECT PEACE, WHOSE MIND IS STAYED ON THEE: BECAUSE HE TRUSTETH IN THEE.**

2 ½ CUPS WATER
> ISAIAH 54:17 **NO WEAPON THAT IS FORMED AGAINST THEE SHALL PROSPER; AND EVERY TONGUE THAT SHALL RISE AGAINST THEE IN JUDGMENT THOU SHALT CONDEMN.**

4 TBSP SUGAR
> PSALM 37:1 **FRET NOT THYSELF BECAUSE OF EVIL DOERS, NEITHER BE THOU ENVIOUS AGAINST THE WORKERS OF INIQUITY.**

1 TSP SALT
> PROVERBS 1:5 **A WISE MAN WILL HEAR, AND WILL INCREASE LEARNING; AND A MAN OF UNDERSTANDING SHALL ATTAIN UNTO WISE COUNSELS.**

5 EGGS
> PROVERBS 15:1 **A SOFT ANSWER TURNETH AWAY WRATH: BUT GRIEVOUS WORDS STIR UP ANGER.**

*ALLOW JESUS TO MIX ALL INGREDIENTS AND BAKE THEM IN GOD'S OVEN UNTIL THE LORD SAYS... "WELL DONE" THY GOOD AND FAITHFUL SERVANT.
- MATTHEW 25:21

Eric Richard Williams

GOD'S RECIPE...
LONELINESS CAKE

3 CUPS FLOUR
   PSALM 3:6 **I WILL NOT BE AFRAID OF TEN THOUSANDS OF PEOPLE, THAT HAVE SET THEMSELVES AGAINST ME ROUND ABOUT.**

2 ½ CUPS WATER
   PSALM 27:10 **WHEN MY FATHER AND MOTHER FORSAKE ME, THEN THE LORD WILL TAKE ME UP.**

4 TBSP SUGAR
   PSALM 37:25 **I HAVE BEEN YOUNG, AND NOW AM OLD; YET HAVE I NOT SEEN THE RIGHTEOUS FORSAKEN, NOR HIS SEED BEGGING BREAD.**

1 TSP SALT
   1 PETER 5:7 **CASTING ALL YOUR CARE UPON HIM; FOR HE CARETH FOR YOU.**

5 EGGS
   JOHN 14:18 **I WILL NOT LEAVE YOU COMFORTLESS: I WILL COME TO YOU.**

*ALLOW JESUS TO MIX ALL INGREDIENTS AND BAKE THEM IN GOD'S OVEN UNTIL THE LORD SAYS… "WELL DONE" THY GOOD AND FAITHFUL SERVANT.
- MATTHEW 25:21

DIVORCE is a Piece of Cake

GOD'S RECIPE...
FEAR CAKE

3 CUPS FLOUR
PSALM 23:4 **YEA, THOUGH I WALK THROUGH THE VALLEY OF THE SHADOW OF DEATH, I WILL FEAR NO EVIL: FOR THOU ART WITH ME; THY ROD AND THY STAFF THEY COMFORT ME.**

2 ½ CUPS WATER
PSALM 27:1 **THE LORD IS MY LIGHT AND MY SALVATION WHOM SHALL I FEAR? THE LORD IS THE STRENGTH OF MY LIFE; OF WHOM SHALL I BE AFRAID?**

4 TBSP SUGAR
PSALM 27:3 **THOUGH AN HOST SHOULD ENCAMP AGAINST ME, MY HEART SHALL NOT FEAR: THOUGH WAR SHOULD RISE AGAINST ME, IN THIS WILL I BE CONFIDENT.**

1 TSP SALT
2 TIMOTHY 1:7 **FOR GOD HATH NOT GIVEN US THE SPIRIT OF FEAR; BUT OF POWER, AND OF LOVE, AND OF A SOUND MIND.**

5 EGGS
DEUTERONOMY 31:6 **BE STRONG AND OF A GOOD COURAGE, FEAR NOT, NOR BE AFRAID OF THEM:**

*ALLOW JESUS TO MIX ALL INGREDIENTS AND BAKE THEM IN GOD'S OVEN UNTIL THE LORD SAYS... "WELL DONE" THY GOOD AND FAITHFUL SERVANT.
- MATTHEW 25:21

Eric Richard Williams

GOD'S RECIPE...
SUICIDE CAKE

3 CUPS FLOUR
PSALM 118:17 **I SHALL NOT DIE, BUT LIVE, AND DECLARE THE WORKS OF THE LORD.**

2 ½ CUPS WATER
JAMES 1:12 **BLESSED IS THE MAN THAT ENDURETH TEMPTATION: FOR WHEN HE IS TRIED, HE SHALL RECEIVE THE CROWN OF LIFE, WHICH THE LORD HATH PROMISED TO THEM THAT LOVE HIM.**

4 TBSP SUGAR
2 CORINTHIANS 10:5 **CASTING DOWN IMAGINATIONS, AND EVERY HIGH THING THAT EXALTETH ITSELF AGAINST THE KNOWLEDGE OF GOD, AND BRINGING INTO CAPTIVITY EVERY THOUGHT TO THE OBEDIENCE OF CHRIST.**

1 TSP SALT
ISAIAH 26:3 **THOU WILT KEEP HIM IN PERFECT PEACE, WHOSE MIND IS STAYED ON THEE: BECAUSE HE TRUSTETH IN THEE.**

5 EGGS
PSALM 94:17 **UNLESS THE LORD HAD BEEN MY HELP, MY SOUL HAD ALMOST DWELT IN SILENCE.**

*ALLOW JESUS TO MIX ALL INGREDIENTS AND BAKE THEM IN GOD'S OVEN UNTIL THE LORD SAYS... "WELL DONE" THY GOOD AND FAITHFUL SERVANT.
- MATTHEW 25:21

GOD'S RECIPE...
POSITIVE ATTITUDE CAKE

3 CUPS FLOUR
> PROVERBS 15:13 **A MERRY HEART MAKETH A CHEERFUL COUNTENANCE: BUT BY SORROW OF THE HEART THE SPIRIT IS BROKEN.**

2 ½ CUPS WATER
> PROVERBS 17:22 **A MERRY HEART DOETH GOOD LIKE A MEDICINE: BUT A BROKEN SPIRIT DRIETH THE BONES.**

4 TBSP SUGAR
> JOHN 15:11 **THESE THINGS HAVE I SPOKEN UNTO YOU, THAT MY JOY MIGHT REMAIN IN YOU, AND THAT YOUR JOY MIGHT BE FULL.**

1 TSP SALT
> JAMES 1:2 **MY BRETHREN COUNT IT ALL JOY WHEN YE FALL INTO DIVERS TEMPTATIONS.**

5 EGGS
> PROVERBS 3:13 **HAPPY IS THE MAN THAT FINDETH WISDOM AND THE MAN THAT GETTETH UNDERSTANDING.**

*ALLOW JESUS TO MIX ALL INGREDIENTS AND BAKE THEM IN GOD'S OVEN UNTIL THE LORD SAYS... "WELL DONE" THY GOOD AND FAITHFUL SERVANT.
- MATTHEW 25:21

Eric Richard Williams

GOD'S RECIPE...
MOTIVATION CAKE

3 CUPS FLOUR
> PROVERBS 10:4 **HE BECOMETH POOR THAT DEALETH WITH A SLACK HAND: BUT THE HAND OF THE DILIGENT MAKETH RICH.**

2 ½ CUPS WATER
> PROVERBS 12:11 **HE THAT TILLETH HIS LAND SHALL BE SATISFIED WITH BREAD: BUT HE THAT FOLLOWETH VAIN PERSONS IS VOID OF UNDERSTANDING.**

4 TBSP SUGAR
> PROVERBS 10:5 **HE THAT GATHERETH IN SUMMER IS A WISE SON: BUT HE THAT SLEEPETH IN HARVEST IS A SON THAT CAUSETH SHAME.**

1 TSP SALT
> PROVERBS 12:24 **THE HAND OF THE DILIGENT SHALL BEAR RULE: BUT THE SLOTHFUL SHALL BE UNDER TRIBUTE.**

5 EGGS
> HEBREWS 6:12 **THAT YE BE NOT SLOTHFUL, BUT FOLLOWERS OF THEM WHO THROUGH FAITH AND PATIENCE INHERIT THE PROMISES.**

*ALLOW JESUS TO MIX ALL INGREDIENTS AND BAKE THEM IN GOD'S OVEN UNTIL THE LORD SAYS... "WELL DONE" THY GOOD AND FAITHFUL SERVANT.
- MATTHEW 25:21

GOD'S RECIPE...
HEALING CAKE

3 CUPS FLOUR
PSALM 118:17 **I SHALL NOT DIE, BUT LIVE, AND DECLARE THE WORKS OF THE LORD.**

2 ½ CUPS WATER
PSALM 91:16 **WITH LONG LIFE WILL I SATISFY HIM, AND SHOW HIM MY SALVATION.**

4 TBSP SUGAR
PSALM 107:20 **HE SENT HIS WORD, AND HEALED THEM, AND DELIVERED THEM FROM THEIR DESTRUCTIONS.**

1 TSP SALT
JAMES 5:15 **AND THE PRAYER OF FAITH SHALL SAVE THE SICK, AND THE LORD SHALL RAISE HIM UP; AND IF HE HAVE COMMITTED SINS, THEY SHALL BE FORGIVEN HIM.**

5 EGGS
ISAIAH 53:5 **BUT HE WAS WOUNDED FOR OUR TRANSGRESSIONS, HE WAS BRUISED FOR OUR INIQUITIES: THE CHASTISEMENT OF OUR PEACE WAS UPON HIM; AND WITH HIS STRIPES WE ARE HEALED.**

*ALLOW JESUS TO MIX ALL INGREDIENTS AND BAKE THEM IN GOD'S OVEN UNTIL THE LORD SAYS... "WELL DONE" THY GOOD AND FAITHFUL SERVANT.
- MATTHEW 25:21

Eric Richard Williams

GOD'S RECIPE...
PROTECTION CAKE

3 CUPS FLOUR
　　PSALM 46:1 **GOD IS OUR REFUGE AND STRENGTH, A VERY PRESENT HELP IN TROUBLE.**

2 ½ CUPS WATER
　　JUDE 24 **NOW UNTO HIM THAT IS ABLE TO KEEP YOU FROM FALLING, AND TO PRESENT YOU FAULTLESS BEFORE THE PRESENCE OF HIS GLORY WITH EXCEEDING JOY.**

4 TBSP SUGAR
　　PSALM 32:7 **THOU ART MY HIDING PLACE; THOU SHALT PRESERVE ME FROM TROUBLE, THOU SHALT COMPASS ME ABOUT WITH SONGS OF DELIVERANCE. SELAH.**

1 TSP SALT
　　PSALM 18:17 **HE DELIVERED ME FROM MY STRONG ENEMY, AND FROM THEM WHICH HATED ME: FOR THEY WERE TOO STRONG FOR ME.**

5 EGGS
　　PSALM 60:11 **GIVE US HELP FROM TROUBLE: FOR VAIN IS THE HELP OF MAN.**

*ALLOW JESUS TO MIX ALL INGREDIENTS AND BAKE THEM IN GOD'S OVEN UNTIL THE LORD SAYS... "WELL DONE" THY GOOD AND FAITHFUL SERVANT.
- MATTHEW 25:21

GOD'S RECIPE...
LOVE CAKE

3 CUPS FLOUR
> JOHN 3:16 **FOR GOD SO LOVED THE WORLD, THAT HE GAVE HIS ONLY BEGOTTEN SON, THAT WHOSOEVER BELIEVETH IN HIM SHOULD NOT PERISH, BUT HAVE EVERLASTING LIFE.**

2 ½ CUPS WATER
> PSALM 116:1 **I LOVE THE LORD, BECAUSE HE HATH HEARD MY VOICE AND MY SUPPLICATIONS.**

4 TBSP SUGAR
> PROVERBS 10:12 **HATRED STIRRETH UP STRIFES: BUT LOVE COVERETH ALL SINS.**

1 TSP SALT
> PROVERBS 17:17 **A FRIEND LOVETH AT ALL TIMES, AND A BROTHER IS BORN FOR ADVERSITY.**

5 EGGS
> JOHN 13:35 **BY THIS SHALL ALL MEN KNOW THAT YE ARE MY DISCIPLES, IF YE HAVE LOVE FOR ONE ANOTHER.**

*ALLOW JESUS TO MIX ALL INGREDIENTS AND BAKE THEM IN GOD'S OVEN UNTIL THE LORD SAYS... "WELL DONE" THY GOOD AND FAITHFUL SERVANT.
- MATTHEW 25:21

Eric Richard Williams

GOD'S RECIPE...
STRENGTH CAKE

3 CUPS FLOUR
    2 SAMUEL 22:33 **GOD IS MY STRENGTH AND POWER: AND HE MAKETH MY WAY PERFECT.**

2 ½ CUPS WATER
    PSALM 19:14 **LET THE WORDS OF MY MOUTH, AND THE MEDITATION OF MY HEART, BE ACCEPTABLE IN THY SIGHT, O LORD, MY STRENGTH, AND MY REDEEMER.**

4 TBSP SUGAR
    EPHESIANS 6:10 **FINALLY MY BRETHREN, BE STRONG IN THE LORD, AND IN THE POWER OF HIS MIGHT.**

1 TSP SALT
    ISAIAH 40:29 **HE GIVETH POWER TO THE FAINT; AND TO THEM THAT HAVE NO MIGHT HE INCREASETH STRENGTH.**

5 EGGS
    PSALM 118:14 **THE LORD IS MY STRENGTH AND SONG, AND IS BECOME MY SALVATION.**

*ALLOW JESUS TO MIX ALL INGREDIENTS AND BAKE THEM IN GOD'S OVEN UNTIL THE LORD SAYS... "WELL DONE" THY GOOD AND FAITHFUL SERVANT.
- MATTHEW 25:21

GOD'S RECIPE...
ENEMY CAKE

3 CUPS FLOUR
> PSALM 25:2 **O MY GOD, I TRUST IN THEE: LET ME NOT BE ASHAMED, LET NOT MINE ENEMIES TRIUMPH OVER ME.**

2 ½ CUPS WATER
> PSALM 37:13 **THE LORD SHALL LAUGH AT THE WICKED: FOR HE SEETH HIS DAY COMING.**

4 TBSP SUGAR
> PSALM 110:1 **THE LORD SAID UNTO MY LORD, SIT THOU AT MY RIGHT HAND, UNTIL I MAKE THINE ENEMIES THY FOOTSTOOL.**

1 TSP SALT
> PSALM 37:17 **FOR THE ARMS OF THE WICKED SHALL BE BROKEN: BUT THE LORD UPHOLDETH THE RIGHTEOUS.**

5 EGGS
> ISAIAH 54:17 **NO WEAPON THAT IS FORMED AGAINST THEE SHALL PROSPER; AND EVERY TONGUE THAT SHALL RISE AGAINST THEE IN JUDGMENT THOU SHALT CONDEMN.**

*ALLOW JESUS TO MIX ALL INGREDIENTS AND BAKE THEM IN GOD'S OVEN UNTIL THE LORD SAYS... "WELL DONE" THY GOOD AND FAITHFUL SERVANT.
- MATTHEW 25:21

Eric Richard Williams

GOD'S RECIPE...
RAISING YOUR CHILD CAKE

3 CUPS FLOUR
   PROVERBS 22:6 **TRAIN UP A CHILD IN THE WAY HE SHOULD GO: AND WHEN HE IS OLD, HE WILL NOT DEPART FROM IT.**

2 ½ CUPS WATER
   EPHESIANS 6:4 **AND, YE FATHERS, PROVOKE NOT YOUR CHILDREN TO WRATH: BUT BRING THEM UP IN THE NURTURE AND ADMONITION OF THE LORD.**

4 TBSP SUGAR
   PROVERBS 22:15 **FOOLISHNESS IS BOUND IN THE HEART OF A CHILD; BUT THE ROD OF CORRECTION SHALL DRIVE IT FAR FROM HIM.**

1 TSP SALT
   PROVERBS 15:1 **A SOFT ANSWER TURNETH AWAY WRATH: BUT GRIEVOUS WORDS STIR UP ANGER.**

5 EGGS
   GALATIANS 6:9 **AND LET US NOT BE WEARY IN WELL DOING: FOR IN DUE SEASON WE SHALL REAP, IF WE FAINT NOT.**

*ALLOW JESUS TO MIX ALL INGREDIENTS AND BAKE THEM IN GOD'S OVEN UNTIL THE LORD SAYS… "WELL DONE" THY GOOD AND FAITHFUL SERVANT.
- MATTHEW 25:21

DIVORCE is a Piece of Cake

GOD'S RECIPE...
CHEATED ON CAKE

3 CUPS FLOUR
GALATIANS 6:7 **BE NOT DECEIVED; GOD IS NOT MOCKED: FOR WHATSOEVER A MAN SOWETH, THAT SHALL HE ALSO REAP.**

2 ½ CUPS WATER
PSALM 37:1 **FRET NOT THYSELF BECAUSE OF EVIL DOERS, NEITHER BE THOU ENVIOUS AGAINST THE WORKERS OF INIQUITY.**

4 TBSP SUGAR
PSALM 27:10 **WHEN MY FATHER AND MOTHER FORSAKE ME, THEN THE LORD WILL TAKE ME UP.**

1 TSP SALT
PSALM 30:5 **WEEPING MAY ENDURE FOR A NIGHT, BUT JOY COMETH IN THE MORNING.**

5 EGGS
PSALM 37:8 **CEASE FROM ANGER, AND FORSAKE WRATH: FRET NOT THYSELF IN ANY WISE TO DO EVIL.**

*ALLOW JESUS TO MIX ALL INGREDIENTS AND BAKE THEM IN GOD'S OVEN UNTIL THE LORD SAYS... "WELL DONE" THY GOOD AND FAITHFUL SERVANT.
- MATTHEW 25:21

Eric Richard Williams

GOD'S RECIPE...
REJECTION CAKE

3 CUPS FLOUR
> PSALM 27:10 **WHEN MY FATHER AND MY MOTHER FORSAKE ME, THEN THE LORD WILL TAKE ME UP.**

2 ½ CUPS WATER
> 1 SAMUEL 12:22 **FOR THE LORD WILL NOT FORSAKE HIS PEOPLE FOR HIS GREAT NAMES SAKE: BECAUSE IT HATH PLEASED THE LORD TO MAKE YOU HIS PEOPLE.**

4 TBSP SUGAR
> PSALM 94:14 **FOR THE LORD WILL NOT CAST OFF HIS PEOPLE, NEITHER WILL HE FORSAKE HIS INHERITANCE.**

1 TSP SALT
> PSALM 9:10 **AND THEY THAT KNOW THY NAME WILL PUT THEIR TRUST IN THEE; FOR THOU, LORD, HAS NOT FORSAKEN THEM THAT SEEK THEE.**

5 EGGS
> PSALM 30:5 **WEEPING MAY ENDURE FOR A NIGHT, BUT JOY COMETH IN THE MORNING.**

*ALLOW JESUS TO MIX ALL INGREDIENTS AND BAKE THEM IN GOD'S OVEN UNTIL THE LORD SAYS... "WELL DONE" THY GOOD AND FAITHFUL SERVANT.
- MATTHEW 25:21

DIVORCE is a Piece of Cake

GOD'S RECIPE...
BANKRUPTCY CAKE

3 CUPS FLOUR
> PHILIPPIANS 4:19 **BUT MY GOD SHALL SUPPLY ALL YOUR NEED ACCORDING TO HIS RICHES IN GLORY BY CHRIST JESUS.**

2 ½ CUPS WATER
> 3 JOHN: 2 **BELOVED, I WISH ABOVE ALL THINGS THAT THOU MAYEST PROSPER AND BE IN HEALTH, EVEN AS THY SOUL PROSPERETH.**

4 TBSP SUGAR
> PROVERBS 10:22 **THE BLESSING OF THE LORD, IT MAKETH RICH, AND HE ADDETH NO SORROW WITH IT.**

1 TSP SALT
> PROVERBS 24:10 **IF THOU FAINT IN THE DAY OF ADVERSITY, THY STRENGTH IS SMALL.**

5 EGGS
> PSALM 9:18 **FOR THE NEEDY SHALL NOT ALWAYS BE FORGOTTEN: THE EXPECTATION OF THE POOR SHALL NOT PERISH FOREVER.**

*ALLOW JESUS TO MIX ALL INGREDIENTS AND BAKE THEM IN GOD'S OVEN UNTIL THE LORD SAYS… "WELL DONE" THY GOOD AND FAITHFUL SERVANT.
- MATTHEW 25:21

Eric Richard Williams

GOD'S RECIPE...
OVERCOMER CAKE

3 CUPS FLOUR
ROMANS 12:21 **BE NOT OVERCOME OF EVIL, BUT OVERCOME EVIL WITH GOOD.**

2 ½ CUPS WATER
ROMANS 8:37 **WE ARE MORE THAN CONQUERORS THROUGH HIM THAT LOVED US.**

4 TBSP SUGAR
JOHN 4:4 **YE ARE OF GOD, LITTLE CHILDREN, AND HAVE OVERCOME THEM: BECAUSE GREATER IS HE THAT IS IN YOU, THAN HE THAT IS IN THE WORLD.**

1 TSP SALT
1 CORINTHIANS 15:57 **THANKS BE TO GOD WHICH GIVETH US THE VICTORY THROUGH OUR LORD JESUS CHRIST.**

5 EGGS
REVALATION 21:7 **HE THAT OVERCOMETH SHALL INHERIT ALL THINGS; AND I WILL BE HIS GOD, AND HE WILL BE MY SON.**

*ALLOW JESUS TO MIX ALL INGREDIENTS AND BAKE THEM IN GOD'S OVEN UNTIL THE LORD SAYS… "WELL DONE" THY GOOD AND FAITHFUL SERVANT.
- MATTHEW 25:21

GOD'S RECIPE...
DEPRESSION CAKE

3 CUPS FLOUR
PSALM 30:5 **WEEPING MAY ENDURE FOR A NIGHT, BUT JOY COMETH IN THE MORNING.**

2 ½ CUPS WATER
PSALM 34:17 **THE RIGHTEOUS CRY, AND THE LORD HEARETH, AND DELIVERETH THEM OUT OF ALL OF THEIR TROUBLES.**

4 TBSP SUGAR
PSALM 147:3 **HE HEALETH THE BROKEN IN HEART, AND BINDETH UP THEIR WOUNDS.**

1 TSP SALT
ISAIAH 40:31 **BUT THEY THAT WAIT UPON THE LORD SHALL RENEW THEIR STRENGTH; THEY SHALL MOUNT UP WITH WINGS AS EAGLES; THEY SHALL RUN, AND NOT BE WEARY; AND THEY SHALL WALK AND NOT FAINT.**

5 EGGS
PSALM 33:18 **BEHOLD, THE EYE OF THE LORD IS UPON THEM THAT FEAR HIM, UPON THEM THAT HOPE IN HIS MERCY.**

*ALLOW JESUS TO MIX ALL INGREDIENTS AND BAKE THEM IN GOD'S OVEN UNTIL THE LORD SAYS... "WELL DONE" THY GOOD AND FAITHFUL SERVANT.
- MATTHEW 25:21

Eric Richard Williams

GOD'S RECIPE...
CRISIS CAKE

3 CUPS FLOUR
> PSALM 34:4 **I SOUGHT THE LORD, AND HE HEARD ME, AND DELIVERED ME FROM ALL OF MY FEARS.**

2 ½ CUPS WATER
> PSALM 46:10 **BE STILL, AND KNOW THAT I AM GOD: I WILL BE EXALTED AMONG THE HEATHEN, I WILL BE EXALTED IN THE EARTH.**

4 TBSP SUGAR
> PSALM 62:11 **GOD HAS SPOKEN ONCE; TWICE HAVE I HEARD THIS; THAT POWER BELONGETH UNTO GOD.**

1 TSP SALT
> LUKE 21:19 **IN YOUR PATIENCE POSSESS YE YOUR SOULS.**

5 EGGS
> JOHN 14:18 **I WILL NOT LEAVE YOU COMFORTLESS: I WILL COME TO YOU.**

*ALLOW JESUS TO MIX ALL INGREDIENTS AND BAKE THEM IN GOD'S OVEN UNTIL THE LORD SAYS... "WELL DONE" THY GOOD AND FAITHFUL SERVANT.
- MATTHEW 25:21

GOD'S RECIPE...
BROKEN HEART CAKE

3 CUPS FLOUR
PSALM 34:18 **THE LORD IS NIGH UNTO THEM THAT ARE OF A BROKEN HEART; AND SAVETH SUCH AS BE OF A CONTRITE SPIRIT.**

2 ½ CUPS WATER
PSALM 107:20 **HE SENT HIS WORD, AND HEALED THEM, AND DELIVERED THEM FROM THEIR DESTRUCTIONS.**

4 TBSP SUGAR
PSALM 147:3 **HE HEALETH THE BROKEN IN HEART AND BINDETH UP THEIR WOUNDS.**

1 TSP SALT
ISAIAH 53:5 **BUT HE WAS WOUNDED FOR OUR TRANSGRESSIONS, HE WAS BRUISED FOR OUR INIQUITIES: THE CHASTISEMENT OF OUR PEACE WAS UPON HIM AND WITH HIS STRIPES WE ARE HEALED.**

5 EGGS
PSALM 118:17 **I SHALL NOT DIE, BUT LIVE, AND DECLARE THE WORKS OF THE LORD.**

*ALLOW JESUS TO MIX ALL INGREDIENTS AND BAKE THEM IN GOD'S OVEN UNTIL THE LORD SAYS... "WELL DONE" THY GOOD AND FAITHFUL SERVANT.
- MATTHEW 25:21

Eric Richard Williams

GOD'S RECIPE...
PEACE CAKE

3 CUPS FLOUR
> PSALM 37:37 **MARK THE PERFECT MAN, AND BEHOLD THE UPRIGHT: FOR THE END OF THAT MAN IS PEACE.**

2 ½ CUPS WATER
> PROVERBS 16:7 **WHEN A MAN'S WAYS PLEASE THE LORD, HE MAKETH EVEN HIS ENEMIES TO BE AT PEACE WITH HIM.**

4 TBSP SUGAR
> MATTHEW 5:9 **BLESSED ARE THE PEACEMAKERS: FOR THEY SHALL BE CALLED THE CHILDREN OF GOD.**

1 TSP SALT
> ROMANS 5:1 **THEREFORE BEING JUSTIFIED BY FAITH, WE HAVE PEACE WITH GOD THROUGH OUR LORD JESUS CHRIST.**

5 EGGS
> JOB 22:21 **ACQUAINT NOW THYSELF WITH HIM, AND BE AT PEACE: THEREBY GOOD SHALL COME UNTO THEE.**

*ALLOW JESUS TO MIX ALL INGREDIENTS AND BAKE THEM IN GOD'S OVEN UNTIL THE LORD SAYS... "WELL DONE" THY GOOD AND FAITHFUL SERVANT.
- MATTHEW 25:21

DIVORCE is a Piece of Cake

GOD'S RECIPE...
PATIENCE CAKE

3 CUPS FLOUR
ROMANS 5:3 **AND NOT ONLY SO, BUT WE GLORY IN TRIBULATIONS ALSO: KNOWING THAT TRIBULATION WORKETH PATIENCE.**

2 ½ CUPS WATER
GALATIANS 6:9 **AND LET US NOT BE WEARY IN WELL DOING: FOR IN DUE SEASON WE SHALL REAP, IF WE FAINT NOT.**

4 TBSP SUGAR
PSALM 37:9 **FOR EVILDOERS SHALL BE CUT OFF: BUT THOSE THAT WAIT UPON THE LORD, THEY SHALL INHERIT THE EARTH.**

1 TSP SALT
JAMES 1:3 **KNOWING THIS, THAT THE TRYING OF YOUR FAITH WORKETH PATIENCE.**

5 EGGS
LUKE 21:19 **IN YOUR PATIENCE POSSESS YE YOUR SOULS.**

*ALLOW JESUS TO MIX ALL INGREDIENTS AND BAKE THEM IN GOD'S OVEN UNTIL THE LORD SAYS… "WELL DONE" THY GOOD AND FAITHFUL SERVANT.
- MATTHEW 25:21

Eric Richard Williams

GOD'S RECIPE...
JOY CAKE

3 CUPS FLOUR
> JOHN 15:11 **THESE THINGS HAVE I SPOKEN UNTO YOU, THAT MY JOY MIGHT REMAIN IN YOU, AND THAT YOUR JOY MIGHT BE FULL.**

2 ½ CUPS WATER
> PSALM 100:1 **MAKE A JOYFUL NOISE UNTO THE LORD, ALL YE LANDS.**

4 TBSP SUGAR
> PSALM 35:9 **AND MY SOUL SHALL BE JOYFUL IN THE LORD: IT SHALL REJOICE IN HIS SALVATION.**

1 TSP SALT
> PSALM 16:11 **THOU WILT SHEW ME THE PATH OF LIFE: IN THY PRESENCE IS FULNESS OF JOY; AT THY RIGHT HAND THERE ARE PLEASURES FOR EVERMORE.**

5 EGGS
> PSALM 9:2 **I WILL BE GLAD AND REJOICE IN THEE: I WILL SING PRAISE TO THY NAME, O THOU MOST HIGH.**

*ALLOW JESUS TO MIX ALL INGREDIENTS AND BAKE THEM IN GOD'S OVEN UNTIL THE LORD SAYS… "WELL DONE" THY GOOD AND FAITHFUL SERVANT.
- MATTHEW 25:21

GOD'S RECIPE...
FALSE ACCUSATION CAKE

3 CUPS FLOUR
> ISAIAH 54:17 **NO WEAPON THAT IS FORMED AGAINST THEE SHALL PROSPER; AND EVERY TONGUE THAT SHALL RISE AGAINST THEE IN JUDGMENT THOU SHALT CONDEMN.**

2 ½ CUPS WATER
> NAHUM 1:7 **THE LORD IS GOOD, A STRONGHOLD IN THE DAY OF TROUBLE; AND HE KNOWETH THEM THAT TRUST IN HIM.**

4 TBSP SUGAR
> MATTHEW 5:11 **BLESSED ARE YE, WHEN MEN SHALL REVILE YOU, AND PERSECUTE YOU, AND SHALL SAY ALL MANNER OF EVIL AGAINST YOU FALSELY, FOR MY SAKE.**

1 TSP SALT
> MARK 14:56 **FOR MANY BARE FALSE WITNESS AGAINST HIM, BUT THEIR WITNESS AGREED NOT TOGETHER.**

5 EGGS
> LUKE 10:19 **BEHOLD, I GIVE YOU POWER TO TREAD ON SERPENTS AND SCORPIONS, AND OVER ALL THE POWER OF THE ENEMY: AND NOTHING SHALL BY ANY MEANS HURT YOU.**

*ALLOW JESUS TO MIX ALL INGREDIENTS AND BAKE THEM IN GOD'S OVEN UNTIL THE LORD SAYS... "WELL DONE" THY GOOD AND FAITHFUL SERVANT.
- MATTHEW 25:21

Eric Richard Williams

GOD'S RECIPE...
ENCOURAGEMENT CAKE

3 CUPS FLOUR
   PSALM 31:24 **BE OF GOOD COURAGE, AND HE SHALL STRENGTHEN YOUR HEART, ALL YE THAT HOPE IN THE LORD.**

2 ½ CUPS WATER
   PSALM 30:5 **WEEPING MAY ENDURE FOR A NIGHT, BUT JOY COMETH IN THE MORNING.**

4 TBSP SUGAR
   PHILIPPIANS 4:19 **BUT MY GOD SHALL SUPPLY ALL YOUR NEED ACCORDING TO HIS RICHES IN GLORY BY CHRIST JESUS.**

1 TSP SALT
   1 PETER 5:7 **CASTING ALL YOUR CARE UPON HIM; FOR HE CARETH FOR YOU.**

5 EGGS
   PSALM 147:3 **HE HEALETH THE BROKEN IN HEART, AND BINDETH UP THEIR WOUNDS.**

*ALLOW JESUS TO MIX ALL INGREDIENTS AND BAKE THEM IN GOD'S OVEN UNTIL THE LORD SAYS... "WELL DONE" THY GOOD AND FAITHFUL SERVANT.
- MATTHEW 25:21

GOD'S RECIPE...
FAITH CAKE

3 CUPS FLOUR
 HEBREWS 11:1 **NOW FAITH IS THE SUBSTANCE OF THINGS HOPED FOR, THE EVIDENCE OF THINGS NOT SEEN.**

2 ½ CUPS WATER
 HEBREWS 11:6 **BUT WITHOUT FAITH IT IS IMPOSSIBLE TO PLEASE HIM.**

4 TBSP SUGAR
 JAMES 2:17 **EVEN SO FAITH, IF IT HATH NOT WORKS, IS DEAD, BEING ALONE.**

1 TSP SALT
 2 CORINTHIANS 5:7 **FOR WE WALK BY FAITH, NOT BY SIGHT.**

5 EGGS
 MARK 9:23 **JESUS SAID UNTO HIM, IF THOU CANST BELIEVE, ALL THINGS ARE POSSIBLE TO HIM THAT BELIEVETH.**

*ALLOW JESUS TO MIX ALL INGREDIENTS AND BAKE THEM IN GOD'S OVEN UNTIL THE LORD SAYS… "WELL DONE" THY GOOD AND FAITHFUL SERVANT.
 - MATTHEW 25:21

Eric Richard Williams

GOD'S RECIPE...
ANGER CAKE

3 CUPS FLOUR
   PROVERBS 20:3 **IT IS AN HONOR FOR A MAN TO CEASE FROM STRIFE: BUT EVERY FOOL WILL BE MEDDLING.**

2 ½ CUPS WATER
   PSALM 37:8 **CEASE FROM ANGER, AND FORSAKE WRATH: FRET NOT THYSELF IN ANY WISE TO DO EVIL.**

4 TBSP SUGAR
   ECCLESIASTES 7:9 **BE NOT HASTY IN THY SPIRIT TO BE ANGRY: FOR ANGER RESTETH IN THE BOSOM OF FOOLS.**

1 TSP SALT
   MATTHEW 5:9 **BLESSED ARE THE PEACEMAKERS: FOR THEY SHALL BE CALLED THE CHILDREN OF GOD.**

5 EGGS
   GALATIANS 6:9 **AND LET US NOT BE WEARY IN WELL DOING: FOR IN DUE SEASON WE SHALL REAP, IF WE FAINT NOT.**

*ALLOW JESUS TO MIX ALL INGREDIENTS AND BAKE THEM IN GOD'S OVEN UNTIL THE LORD SAYS... "WELL DONE" THY GOOD AND FAITHFUL SERVANT.
- MATTHEW 25:21

GOD'S RECIPE...
HELP CAKE

3 CUPS FLOUR
   PSALM 46:1 **GOD IS OUR REFUGE AND STRENGTH, A VERY PRESENT HELP IN TROUBLE.**

2 ½ CUPS WATER
   PSALM 63:7 **BECAUSE THOU HAST BEEN MY HELP, THEREFORE IN THE SHADOW OF THY WINGS WILL I REJOICE.**

4 TBSP SUGAR
   PSALM 94:17 **UNLESS THE LORD HAD BEEN MY HELP, MY SOUL HAD ALMOST DWELT IN SILENCE.**

1 TSP SALT
   PSALM 121:1 **I WILL LIFT UP MINE EYES, UNTO THE HILLS, FROM WHENCE COMETH MY HELP.**

5 EGGS
   PSALM 121:2 **MY HELP COMETH FROM THE LORD, WHICH MADE HEAVEN AND EARTH.**

*ALLOW JESUS TO MIX ALL INGREDIENTS AND BAKE THEM IN GOD'S OVEN UNTIL THE LORD SAYS... "WELL DONE" THY GOOD AND FAITHFUL SERVANT.
   - MATTHEW 25:21

Eric Richard Williams

GOD'S RECIPE...
GOOD CAKE

3 CUPS FLOUR
GENESIS 50:20 **BUT AS FOR YOU, YE THOUGHT EVIL AGAINST ME; BUT GOD MEANT IT UNTO GOOD, TO BRING TO PASS, AS IT IS THIS DAY, TO SAVE MUCH PEOPLE ALIVE.**

2 ½ CUPS WATER
PSALM 31:24 **BE OF GOOD COURAGE, AND HE SHALL STRENGTHEN YOUR HEART, ALL YE THAT HOPE IN THE LORD.**

4 TBSP SUGAR
PSALM 34:8 **O TASTE AND SEE THAT THE LORD IS GOOD: BLESSED IS THE MAN THAT TRUSTETH IN HIM.**

1 TSP SALT
PSALM 37:23 **THE STEPS OF A GOOD MAN ARE ORDERED BY THE LORD: AND HE DELIGHTETH IN HIS WAY.**

5 EGGS
PSALM 100:5 **FOR THE LORD IS GOOD; HIS MERCY IS EVERLASTING; AND HIS TRUTH ENDURETH TO ALL GENERATIONS.**

*ALLOW JESUS TO MIX ALL INGREDIENTS AND BAKE THEM IN GOD'S OVEN UNTIL THE LORD SAYS... "WELL DONE" THY GOOD AND FAITHFUL SERVANT.
- MATTHEW 25:21

DIVORCE is a Piece of Cake

GOD'S RECIPE...
DATING AGAIN CAKE

3 CUPS FLOUR
2 TIMOTHY 1:7 **FOR GOD HATH NOT GIVEN US THE SPIRIT OF FEAR; BUT OF POWER, AND OF LOVE, AND OF A SOUND MIND.**

2 ½ CUPS WATER
2 CORINTHIANS 6:14 **BE YE NOT UNEQUALLY YOKED TOGETHER WITH UNBELIEVERS: FOR WHAT FELLOWSHIP HATH RIGHTEOUSNESS WITH UNRIGHTEOUSNESS? AND WHAT COMMUNION HATH LIGHT WITH DARKNESS?**

4 TBSP SUGAR
PROVERBS 3:6 **IN ALL THY WAYS ACKNOWLEDGE HIM, AND HE SHALL DIRECT THY PATHS.**

1 TSP SALT
I CORITHIANS 7:2 **NEVERTHELESS, TO AVOID FORNICATION, LET EVERY MAN HAVE HIS OWN WIFE, AND LET EVERY WOMAN HAVE HER OWN HUSBAND.**

5 EGGS
PSALM 37:4 **DELIGHT THYSELF ALSO IN THE LORD, AND HE SHALL GIVE THEE THE DESIRES OF THINE HEART.**

*ALLOW JESUS TO MIX ALL INGREDIENTS AND BAKE THEM IN GOD'S OVEN UNTIL THE LORD SAYS... "WELL DONE" THY GOOD AND FAITHFUL SERVANT.
- MATTHEW 25:21

Eric Richard Williams

GOD'S RECIPE...
RE-MARRIAGE CAKE

3 CUPS FLOUR
> PHILIPPIANS 3:13 **FORGETTING THOSE THINGS WHICH ARE BEHIND, AND REACHING FORTH UNTO THOSE THINGS WHICH ARE BEFORE.**

2 ½ CUPS WATER
> PROVERBS 18:22 **WHOSO FINDETH A WIFE FINDETH A GOOD THING, AND OBTAINETH FAVOR OF THE LORD.**

4 TBSP SUGAR
> HEBREWS 13:4 **MARRIAGE IS HONORABLE IN ALL, AND THE BED UNDEFILED: BUT WHOREMONGERS AND ADULTERERS GOD WILL JUDGE.**

1 TSP SALT
> EPHESIANS 5:25 **HUSBANDS, LOVE YOUR WIVES, EVEN AS CHRIST ALSO LOVED THE CHURCH, AND GAVE HIMSELF FOR IT.**

5 EGGS
> ISAIAH 43:19 **BEHOLD, I WILL DO A NEW THING; NOW IT SHALL SPRING FORTH; SHALL YE NOT KNOW IT? I WILL EVEN MAKE A WAY IN THE WILDERNESS, AND RIVERS IN THE DESERT.**

*ALLOW JESUS TO MIX ALL INGREDIENTS AND BAKE THEM IN GOD'S OVEN UNTIL THE LORD SAYS... "WELL DONE" THY GOOD AND FAITHFUL SERVANT.
- MATTHEW 25:21

INSPIRATIONAL SLICES

"Divorce is a Piece of Cake"
Inspirational Cookbook on Surviving Divorce
By: Eric Richard Williams

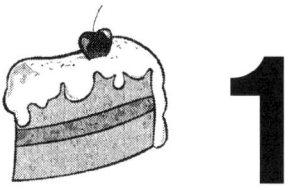

If you can survive a divorce, you can survive anything.

Never let people determine your destiny.

Never be afraid of failing, be afraid of not trying.

"A slice a day keeps the pain away."

Eric Richard Williams

4
God has placed a gift inside of you... unwrap it!

5
Helping someone is always better than hurting anyone.

6
Treat everyone right... including your enemies.

"A slice a day keeps the pain away."

DIVORCE is a Piece of Cake

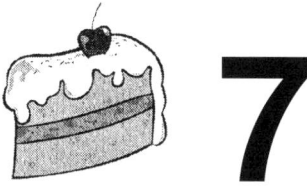

7
Just because you were knocked down doesn't mean you were knocked out.

8
When you have no one else, you always have you.

9
The enemy likes to see you down... so get up!

"A slice a day keeps the pain away."

10

If you don't deal with issues, you will deal with tissues.

11

People who give up never grow up.

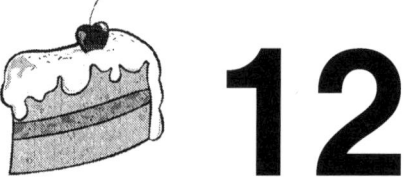

12

Never expect someone to love you if you don't love yourself.

"A slice a day keeps the pain away."

DIVORCE is a Piece of Cake

13
Hurt is like a rubber band, it will hold you back until you let go of it.

14
Never make a long term decision over a short term circumstance.

15
Never trust people with your secrets if they don't trust you with their's.

"A slice a day keeps the pain away."

 **16**

Trust is like money; it should be earned.

 **17**

Just because your marriage is over, doesn't mean your life is over.

 **18**

A marriage is like debt; it's much easier to get into than to get out of.

"A slice a day keeps the pain away."

DIVORCE is a Piece of Cake

 **19**

God takes underdogs and makes them overcomers.

 **20**

If you never learn how to control your mind, you'll never learn how to control your life.

 **21**

Just because your marriage was bad doesn't mean the people in it were bad.

"A slice a day keeps the pain away."

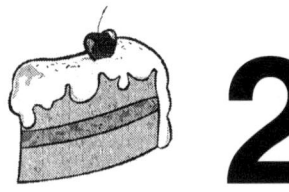 **22**

Never say that you failed at marriage, always say that you survived divorce.

 **23**

The best thing about your past is that it's behind you.

 **24**

Divorce will reveal the difference between relatives and family.

"A slice a day keeps the pain away."

DIVORCE is a Piece of Cake

 **25**

The more you talk about your past is the more you talk yourself out of your future.

 **26**

Most people end up in divorce because they focused more on their wedding than their marriage.

 **27**

The best way to get over a divorce is to help someone else through one.

"A slice a day keeps the pain away."

Eric Richard Williams

28
People who constantly cause you pain are unnecessary in your life.

29
Get your focus off of your "X" and put it on "U".

30
People who walk on you are not qualified to walk with you.

"A slice a day keeps the pain away."

DIVORCE is a Piece of Cake

31
Your enemies get excited about your past; your friends get excited about your future.

32
The only reason you're not over your past is because you keep thinking about it.

33
When wrong people leave your life, right things start to happen in your life.

"A slice a day keeps the pain away."

Eric Richard Williams

Your comeback is going to be better than your setback.

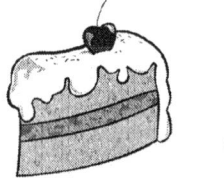

Never try to pay back someone for hurting you... it costs too much.

Never let your situation determine your destination.

"A slice a day keeps the pain away."

DIVORCE is a Piece of Cake

37
The person that hurt you the most will one day need you the most.

38
Why be upset with your past when God has set up your future?

39
Someone may be responsible for breaking your heart, but you're responsible for putting it back together.

"A slice a day keeps the pain away."

Eric Richard Williams

 **40**

Isolation always comes before elevation.

 **41**

Forgiving the person who hurt you doesn't make them right, it makes you free.

 **42**

The Lord and the devil have one thing in common... they both use people.

"A slice a day keeps the pain away."

DIVORCE is a Piece of Cake

 **43**

People who can't relate to your pain tend to judge it.

 **44**

Never judge a person by what they go through, judge them by how they come out.

 **45**

Just because someone hurt you, doesn't mean they hate you.

"A slice a day keeps the pain away."

Eric Richard Williams

Never take your past into your future… there's not enough room.

The only person keeping you from achieving your dreams is you.

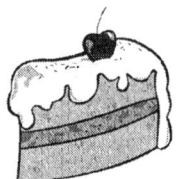

The best thing about being alone is you get to spend time with the most important person in the world.

"A slice a day keeps the pain away."

DIVORCE is a Piece of Cake

 **49**

Why be bitter when God has better?

 **50**

You can't have a testimony without a test.

 **51**

Never breakdown always breakthrough.

"A slice a day keeps the pain away."

52
The only people that can hurt you are those close to you.

53
God will turn your mess into a message.

54
Things that come easily in life usually leave the same way.

"A slice a day keeps the pain away."

DIVORCE is a Piece of Cake

# 55
Learn to like yourself because you'll be with you for the rest of your life.

# 56
If you don't have a game plan, your just playing games.

# 57
The best relationship you'll ever have is with God.

"A slice a day keeps the pain away."

Eric Richard Williams

 **58**

**Communicate with God...
He loves the attention.**

 **59**

**You don't always have control
over what you go through,
but you always have control
over how you go through it.**

 **60**

**Never let a person determine
your value... God has already
declared you priceless.**

"A slice a day keeps the pain away."

DIVORCE is a Piece of Cake

61
Stop trying to understand your past... God understands and that's good enough.

62
Praising God in a painful situation releases the pain.

63
Don't be concerned with the opinions of people... be concerned with your purpose.

"A slice a day keeps the pain away."

Eric Richard Williams

64
God brings you out when you least expect it.

65
Always remember to forget the past.

66
The only person you have the power to change is you.

"A slice a day keeps the pain away."

 **67**

God doesn't trust everybody... neither should you.

 **68**

Falling down is one thing... staying down is another.

 **69**

The best revenge is Godly success.

"A slice a day keeps the pain away."

Eric Richard Williams

 **70**

Why fight your enemies when you have a bodyguard?

 **71**

Marriage is like a bank account, you get out what you put in.

 **72**

**God doesn't like you...
He loves you.**

"A slice a day keeps the pain away."

DIVORCE is a Piece of Cake

 **73**

God is like money; I'd rather have Him and not need Him than need Him and not have Him.

 **74**

God won't stay in a relationship with you if you're having an affair with the devil.

 **75**

It's impossible to look down on people when you're looking up at God.

"A slice a day keeps the pain away."

Eric Richard Williams

 **76**

The enemy doesn't mind you believing God as long as you don't act on what you believe.

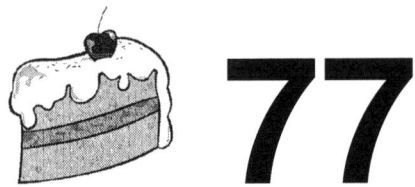 **77**

Minimize those who aggravate you... Maximize those who motivate you.

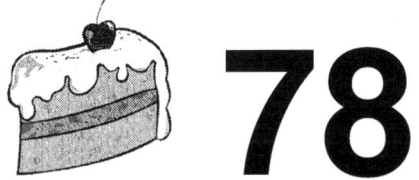 **78**

You're in God's Army... Be all you can be!!

"A slice a day keeps the pain away."

DIVORCE is a Piece of Cake

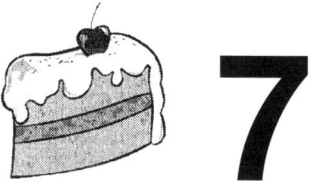 **79**

God never "fails," that's why He's in a "class" by Himself.

 **80**

Change is not change until you change.

 **81**

Reach out to God… He doesn't mind being touched.

"A slice a day keeps the pain away."

Eric Richard Williams

 **82**

**Hearing God is Good...
Listening to God is better.**

 **83**

Never have a "Pity Party" because your guests won't come.

 **84**

People will say that they love you... God will show you.

"A slice a day keeps the pain away."

DIVORCE is a Piece of Cake

85

Don't depend on people to lift your burdens... they're not strong enough.

86

Hard times will humble you.

87

Faith is not natural... it's spiritual.

"A slice a day keeps the pain away."

88
The reason God won't allow people to bring you out is because you would owe them the praise.

89
You're not supposed to see your way out, you're supposed to believe your way out.

90
In order for you to look where God has brought you from, you would need a telescope.

"A slice a day keeps the pain away."

91

A bad marriage is like a tight shoe… it looks good on the outside but it will continue to hurt as long as you stay in it.

92

An enemy will never believe the truth about you, a friend will never believe a lie about you.

93

God always gets the last laugh.

"A slice a day keeps the pain away."

Eric Richard Williams

 **94**

Investing in your past causes bankruptcy; Investing in your future pays dividends.

 **95**

God is like scotch tape, you don't see Him but you know He's holding you together.

 **96**

The worst enemy is the one you're not aware of.

"A slice a day keeps the pain away."

DIVORCE is a Piece of Cake

97
If God allows your enemy to see you in the pit, He's obligated to make sure they see you in the palace.

98
Crying over spilled milk makes you sour.

99
If you lose your mind over your past, God won't have anything to blow in your future.

"A slice a day keeps the pain away."

 **100**

Forgiveness is not a feeling… it's a decision.

 **101**

Faith is the easiest thing to talk, but it's the hardest thing to walk.

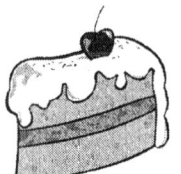 **102**

Talking about your past invites it into your present.

"A slice a day keeps the pain away."

DIVORCE is a Piece of Cake

103
There's never a right time to do a wrong thing.

104
Those who get promotions have learned how to manage their emotions.

105
Godly character is revealed in how you treat someone who hurt you.

"A slice a day keeps the pain away."

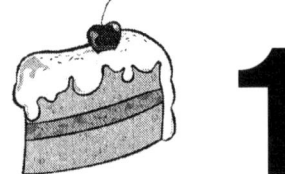
106
You will never fix what you're unwilling to face.

107
People who seek to know your secrets, also seek to reveal them.

108
A divorce is like a car accident, people will slow down to watch you but they won't stop to help you.

"A slice a day keeps the pain away."

DIVORCE is a Piece of Cake

109
The greatest pain is regret.

110
Your greatest deliverance in life is over people.

111
People who are going no where want to take you with them.

"A slice a day keeps the pain away."

Eric Richard Williams

 **112**

No one can feel your pain but you.

 **113**

Never hold a grudge... it weighs too much.

 **114**

You will never overcome what you overlook.

"A slice a day keeps the pain away."

DIVORCE is a Piece of Cake

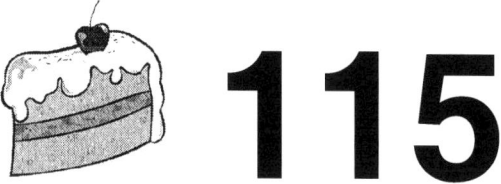
115
You will never overcome those you allow to come over.

116
Heartache is like the winter… it only lasts for a season.

117
Faith will take you into your future, fear will keep you in the past.

"A slice a day keeps the pain away."

Eric Richard Williams

 **118**

There's a difference between where God has brought you from and what He's brought you through.

 **119**

A relationship is like an airport, everyone brings baggage into it.

 **120**

A mistake is like a bed... everyone has made one.

"A slice a day keeps the pain away."

DIVORCE is a Piece of Cake

 **121**

**Anointed people go through...
but they come out.**

 **122**

**People will take advantage
of you, God will give
you the advantage.**

 **123**

**Make friends with God...
You will need him one day.**

"A slice a day keeps the pain away."

124
Never be jealous over what others have, you never know what they had to go through to get it.

125
God will train you in private before he rewards you in public.

126
You can't have faith without focus.

"A slice a day keeps the pain away."

127
Never praise people... appreciate them.

128
Debating with doubters delays your destiny.

129
Behavior that is rewarded is behavior that is repeated.

"A slice a day keeps the pain away."

Eric Richard Williams

 **130**

Divorce is public proof of private problems.

 **131**

Your words create your world.

 **132**

Dealing with people means dealing with imperfection.

"A slice a day keeps the pain away."

133

Poverty is a state of mind not a state of money.

134

You'll never be rich without taking a risk.

135

Your greatest challenge is change.

"A slice a day keeps the pain away."

THE BAKERY

STRAWBERRY "SHORT" CAKE
SHORT TERM GOALS

1. _____

2. _____

3. _____

4. _____

5. _____

6. _____

7. _____

8. _____

9. _____

10. _____

"You can make it if you let God Bake It."

Eric Richard Williams

 # CHOCOLATE "DREAM" CAKE
LONG TERM DREAMS

1. _____
2. _____
3. _____
4. _____
5. _____
6. _____
7. _____
8. _____
9. _____
10. _____

"You can make it if you let God Bake It."

DIVORCE is a Piece of Cake

 # BIRTHDAY CAKE
HOW I WILL CELEBRATE MY NEXT BIRTHDAY

1. _____
2. _____
3. _____
4. _____
5. _____
6. _____
7. _____
8. _____
9. _____
10. _____

"You can make it if you let God Bake It."

Eric Richard Williams

 # FUN-NEL CAKE
FUN THINGS I LIKE TO DO

1. _____

2. _____

3. _____

4. _____

5. _____

6. _____

7. _____

8. _____

9. _____

10. _____

"You can make it if you let God Bake It."

DIVORCE is a Piece of Cake

 # CRAB CAKE
THINGS THAT MAKE ME ANGRY

1. _____

2. _____

3. _____

4. _____

5. _____

6. _____

7. _____

8. _____

9. _____

10. _____

"You can make it if you let God Bake It."

Eric Richard Williams

ANGEL FOOD CAKE
SPECIAL PEOPLE GOD PLACED IN MY LIFE

1. _____

2. _____

3. _____

4. _____

5. _____

6. _____

7. _____

8. _____

9. _____

10. _____

"You can make it if you let God Bake It."

DIVORCE is a Piece of Cake

ICE CREAM CAKE
PEOPLE I NEED TO FORGIVE AND STOP GIVING THE "COLD" SHOULDER

1. _____
2. _____
3. _____
4. _____
5. _____
6. _____
7. _____
8. _____
9. _____
10. _____

"You can make it if you let God Bake It."

Eric Richard Williams

POUND CAKE
MY WEIGHT LOSS GOALS

1. _____

2. _____

3. _____

4. _____

5. _____

6. _____

7. _____

8. _____

9. _____

10. _____

"You can make it if you let God Bake It."

DIVORCE is a Piece of Cake

 # FRUIT CAKE
POOR DECISIONS I MADE IN THE PAST

1. _____

2. _____

3. _____

4. _____

5. _____

6. _____

7. _____

8. _____

9. _____

10. _____

"You can make it if you let God Bake It."

Eric Richard Williams

PANCAKE
THINGS I NEED TO THANK GOD FOR EVERY MORNING

1. _____

2. _____

3. _____

4. _____

5. _____

6. _____

7. _____

8. _____

9. _____

10. _____

"You can make it if you let God Bake It."

DIVORCE is a Piece of Cake

CRUMB CAKE
BIBLE SCRIPTURES THAT KEPT ME FROM CRUMBLING

1. _____

2. _____

3. _____

4. _____

5. _____

6. _____

7. _____

8. _____

9. _____

10. _____

"You can make it if you let God Bake It."

Eric Richard Williams

GOURMET CAKE
NICE THINGS I DESIRE TO HAVE IN LIFE

1. _____

2. _____

3. _____

4. _____

5. _____

6. _____

7. _____

8. _____

9. _____

10. _____

"You can make it if you let God Bake It."

DIVORCE is a Piece of Cake

SPONGE CAKE
NEGATIVE PEOPLE WHO SOAK UP ALL OF MY ENERGY

1. _____

2. _____

3. _____

4. _____

5. _____

6. _____

7. _____

8. _____

9. _____

10. _____

"You can make it if you let God Bake It."

Eric Richard Williams

CHEESECAKE
THINKING ABOUT THESE THINGS MAKES ME SMILE

1. _____

2. _____

3. _____

4. _____

5. _____

6. _____

7. _____

8. _____

9. _____

10. _____

"You can make it if you let God Bake It."

DIVORCE is a Piece of Cake

NUT CAKE
TYPES OF BEHAVIOR I WILL NOT TOLERATE IN MY NEXT RELATIONSHIP

1. _____
2. _____
3. _____
4. _____
5. _____
6. _____
7. _____
8. _____
9. _____
10. _____

"You can make it if you let God Bake It."

Eric Richard Williams

DEVILS FOOD CAKE
AREAS OF PERSONAL WEAKNESS

1. _____

2. _____

3. _____

4. _____

5. _____

6. _____

7. _____

8. _____

9. _____

10. _____

"You can make it if you let God Bake It."

DIVORCE is a Piece of Cake

COFFEE CAKE
REASONS WHY I DESERVE A BREAK

1. ───────────────────────────

2. ───────────────────────────

3. ───────────────────────────

4. ───────────────────────────

5. ───────────────────────────

6. ───────────────────────────

7. ───────────────────────────

8. ───────────────────────────

9. ───────────────────────────

10. ──────────────────────────

"You can make it if you let God Bake It."

Eric Richard Williams

UPSIDE DOWN CAKE
HOW WILL I TURN MY LIFE AROUND

1. _____

2. _____

3. _____

4. _____

5. _____

6. _____

7. _____

8. _____

9. _____

10. _____

"You can make it if you let God Bake It."

DIVORCE is a Piece of Cake

ICING ON THE CAKE
THINGS I LOVE ABOUT MYSELF

1. _____
2. _____
3. _____
4. _____
5. _____
6. _____
7. _____
8. _____
9. _____
10. _____

"You can make it if you let God Bake It."

Eric Richard Williams

TASTY CAKE
THINGS I CAN DO TO MAKE MY "BITTER" SITUATION "TASTE" BETTER

1. _____

2. _____

3. _____

4. _____

5. _____

6. _____

7. _____

8. _____

9. _____

10. _____

"You can make it if you let God Bake It."

DIVORCE is a Piece of Cake

CAKE MIX
PLACES I CAN GO TO "MIX" WITH NEW PEOPLE

1. _____

2. _____

3. _____

4. _____

5. _____

6. _____

7. _____

8. _____

9. _____

10. _____

"You can make it if you let God Bake It."

Eric Richard Williams

RICE CAKE
THINGS I CAN DO TO "LIGHTEN" MY CHILDREN'S LOAD

1. _____

2. _____

3. _____

4. _____

5. _____

6. _____

7. _____

8. _____

9. _____

10. _____

"You can make it if you let God Bake It."

DIVORCE is a Piece of Cake

FISH CAKE
REASONS WHY I MUST KEEP "SWIMMING" AND NOT ALLOW DIVORCE TO CAUSE ME TO "SINK"

1. _____
2. _____
3. _____
4. _____
5. _____
6. _____
7. _____
8. _____
9. _____
10. _____

"You can make it if you let God Bake It."

Eric Richard Williams

CAKE CANDLES
PEOPLE WHO SUPPORTED ME WHEN THINGS WERE "DARK"

1. _____

2. _____

3. _____

4. _____

5. _____

6. _____

7. _____

8. _____

9. _____

10. _____

"You can make it if you let God Bake It."

DIVORCE is a Piece of Cake

 # BAKE SALE
MY FINANCIAL GOALS

1. _____

2. _____

3. _____

4. _____

5. _____

6. _____

7. _____

8. _____

9. _____

10. _____

"You can make it if you let God Bake It."

Eric Richard Williams

CUP CAKE
SMALL THINGS I CAN DO TO HELP OTHERS

1. _____

2. _____

3. _____

4. _____

5. _____

6. _____

7. _____

8. _____

9. _____

10. _____

"You can make it if you let God Bake It."

"CARAT" CAKE
WHAT IS THE CURRENT VALUE OF MY WEDDING RINGS AND WHAT I PLAN TO DO WITH THEM

1. _____
2. _____
3. _____
4. _____
5. _____
6. _____
7. _____
8. _____
9. _____
10. _____

"You can make it if you let God Bake It."

Eric Richard Williams

 # HOMEMADE CAKE
WHAT IS THE CURRENT VALUE OF MY HOME AND WHAT I PLAN TO DO WITH IT

1. _____

2. _____

3. _____

4. _____

5. _____

6. _____

7. _____

8. _____

9. _____

10. _____

"You can make it if you let God Bake It."

DIVORCE is a Piece of Cake

BEEF CAKE
"BEEFS" I NEED TO RESOLVE WITH MY "X" IN A PEACEFUL MANNER

1. _____

2. _____

3. _____

4. _____

5. _____

6. _____

7. _____

8. _____

9. _____

10. _____

"You can make it if you let God Bake It."

Eric Richard Williams

WEDDING CAKE
TYPE OF WEDDING I DESIRE WHEN I REMARRY

1. _____

2. _____

3. _____

4. _____

5. _____

6. _____

7. _____

8. _____

9. _____

10. _____

"You can make it if you let God Bake It."

DIVORCE is a Piece of Cake

BANANA CAKE
REASONS I SHOULD STOP "MONKEYING" AROUND AND MOVE ON WITH MY LIFE

1. _____

2. _____

3. _____

4. _____

5. _____

6. _____

7. _____

8. _____

9. _____

10. _____

"You can make it if you let God Bake It."

Eric Richard Williams

 # WHIPPED CREAM
THINGS I CAN DO TO STAY ON "TOP" OF MY EMOTIONS

1. _____

2. _____

3. _____

4. _____

5. _____

6. _____

7. _____

8. _____

9. _____

10. _____

"You can make it if you let God Bake It."

DIVORCE is a Piece of Cake

NAPKINS
NEGATIVE WORDS I NEED TO "WIPE" OUT OF MY MOUTH

1. _____
2. _____
3. _____
4. _____
5. _____
6. _____
7. _____
8. _____
9. _____
10. _____

"You can make it if you let God Bake It."

CAKE JOURNAL

CAKE JOURNAL

DAY _____ DATE _____

_____
_____
_____
_____
_____
_____
_____
_____
_____
_____
_____
_____
_____
_____
_____
_____
_____
_____
_____
_____

"O TASTE AND SEE THAT THE LORD IS GOOD."
PSALM 34:8

Eric Richard Williams

CAKE JOURNAL

DAY _____ DATE _____

_____
_____
_____
_____
_____
_____
_____
_____
_____
_____
_____
_____
_____
_____
_____
_____
_____
_____
_____
_____

"O TASTE AND SEE THAT THE LORD IS GOOD."
PSALM 34:8

DIVORCE is a Piece of Cake

CAKE JOURNAL

DAY _____ DATE _____

_____
_____
_____
_____
_____
_____
_____
_____
_____
_____
_____
_____
_____
_____
_____
_____
_____
_____
_____

"O TASTE AND SEE THAT THE LORD IS GOOD."
PSALM 34:8

Eric Richard Williams

CAKE JOURNAL

DAY _____ DATE _____

_____
_____
_____
_____
_____
_____
_____
_____
_____
_____
_____
_____
_____
_____
_____
_____
_____
_____
_____
_____

"O TASTE AND SEE THAT THE LORD IS GOOD."
PSALM 34:8

DIVORCE is a Piece of Cake

CAKE JOURNAL

DAY _____ DATE _____

_____
_____
_____
_____
_____
_____
_____
_____
_____
_____
_____
_____
_____
_____
_____
_____
_____
_____
_____

"O TASTE AND SEE THAT THE LORD IS GOOD."
PSALM 34:8

Eric Richard Williams

CAKE JOURNAL

DAY _____ DATE _____

_____
_____
_____
_____
_____
_____
_____
_____
_____
_____
_____
_____
_____
_____
_____
_____
_____
_____

"O TASTE AND SEE THAT THE LORD IS GOOD."
PSALM 34:8

DIVORCE is a Piece of Cake

CAKE JOURNAL

DAY _____ DATE _____

_____
_____
_____
_____
_____
_____
_____
_____
_____
_____
_____
_____
_____
_____
_____
_____
_____
_____
_____

"O TASTE AND SEE THAT THE LORD IS GOOD."
PSALM 34:8

Eric Richard Williams

CAKE JOURNAL

DAY _____ DATE _____

_____
_____
_____
_____
_____
_____
_____
_____
_____
_____
_____
_____
_____
_____
_____
_____
_____
_____
_____

"O TASTE AND SEE THAT THE LORD IS GOOD."
PSALM 34:8

DIVORCE is a Piece of Cake

CAKE JOURNAL

DAY _____ DATE _____

_____
_____
_____
_____
_____
_____
_____
_____
_____
_____
_____
_____
_____
_____
_____
_____
_____
_____
_____
_____

"O TASTE AND SEE THAT THE LORD IS GOOD."
PSALM 34:8

Eric Richard Williams

CAKE JOURNAL

DAY _____ DATE _____

_____
_____
_____
_____
_____
_____
_____
_____
_____
_____
_____
_____
_____
_____
_____
_____
_____
_____
_____
_____
_____
_____

"O TASTE AND SEE THAT THE LORD IS GOOD."
PSALM 34:8

DIVORCE is a Piece of Cake

CAKE JOURNAL

DAY _____ DATE _____

_____
_____
_____
_____
_____
_____
_____
_____
_____
_____
_____
_____
_____
_____
_____
_____
_____
_____

"O TASTE AND SEE THAT THE LORD IS GOOD."
PSALM 34:8

Eric Richard Williams

CAKE JOURNAL

DAY _____ DATE _____

_____
_____
_____
_____
_____
_____
_____
_____
_____
_____
_____
_____
_____
_____
_____
_____
_____
_____
_____

"O TASTE AND SEE THAT THE LORD IS GOOD."
PSALM 34:8

DIVORCE is a Piece of Cake

CAKE JOURNAL

DAY _____ DATE _____

_____
_____
_____
_____
_____
_____
_____
_____
_____
_____
_____
_____
_____
_____
_____
_____
_____
_____
_____

"O TASTE AND SEE THAT THE LORD IS GOOD."
PSALM 34:8

Eric Richard Williams

CAKE JOURNAL

DAY _____ DATE _____

_____
_____
_____
_____
_____
_____
_____
_____
_____
_____
_____
_____
_____
_____
_____
_____
_____
_____
_____
_____

"O TASTE AND SEE THAT THE LORD IS GOOD."
PSALM 34:8

DIVORCE is a Piece of Cake

CAKE JOURNAL

DAY _____ DATE _____

_____
_____
_____
_____
_____
_____
_____
_____
_____
_____
_____
_____
_____
_____
_____
_____
_____
_____
_____
_____

"O TASTE AND SEE THAT THE LORD IS GOOD."
PSALM 34:8

Eric Richard Williams

CAKE JOURNAL

DAY _____ DATE _____

_____
_____
_____
_____
_____
_____
_____
_____
_____
_____
_____
_____
_____
_____
_____
_____
_____
_____
_____

"O TASTE AND SEE THAT THE LORD IS GOOD."
PSALM 34:8

DIVORCE is a Piece of Cake

CAKE JOURNAL

DAY _____ DATE _____

_____
_____
_____
_____
_____
_____
_____
_____
_____
_____
_____
_____
_____
_____
_____
_____
_____
_____
_____

"O TASTE AND SEE THAT THE LORD IS GOOD."
PSALM 34:8

Eric Richard Williams

CAKE JOURNAL

DAY _____ DATE _____

_____
_____
_____
_____
_____
_____
_____
_____
_____
_____
_____
_____
_____
_____
_____
_____
_____
_____
_____
_____

"O TASTE AND SEE THAT THE LORD IS GOOD."
PSALM 34:8

DIVORCE is a Piece of Cake

CAKE JOURNAL

DAY _____ DATE _____

_____
_____
_____
_____
_____
_____
_____
_____
_____
_____
_____
_____
_____
_____
_____
_____
_____
_____

"O TASTE AND SEE THAT THE LORD IS GOOD."
PSALM 34:8

Eric Richard Williams

CAKE JOURNAL

DAY _____ DATE _____

_____
_____
_____
_____
_____
_____
_____
_____
_____
_____
_____
_____
_____
_____
_____
_____
_____
_____
_____
_____

"O TASTE AND SEE THAT THE LORD IS GOOD."
PSALM 34:8

DIVORCE is a Piece of Cake

CAKE JOURNAL

DAY _____ DATE _____

_____
_____
_____
_____
_____
_____
_____
_____
_____
_____
_____
_____
_____
_____
_____
_____
_____
_____
_____
_____

"O TASTE AND SEE THAT THE LORD IS GOOD."
PSALM 34:8

Eric Richard Williams

CAKE JOURNAL

DAY _____ DATE _____

_____
_____
_____
_____
_____
_____
_____
_____
_____
_____
_____
_____
_____
_____
_____
_____
_____
_____
_____
_____
_____

"O TASTE AND SEE THAT THE LORD IS GOOD."
PSALM 34:8

DIVORCE is a Piece of Cake

CAKE JOURNAL

DAY _____ DATE _____

_____
_____
_____
_____
_____
_____
_____
_____
_____
_____
_____
_____
_____
_____
_____
_____
_____
_____
_____
_____

"O TASTE AND SEE THAT THE LORD IS GOOD."
PSALM 34:8

Eric Richard Williams

CAKE JOURNAL

DAY _____ DATE _____

"O TASTE AND SEE THAT THE LORD IS GOOD."
PSALM 34:8

DIVORCE is a Piece of Cake

CAKE JOURNAL

DAY _____ DATE _____

_____
_____
_____
_____
_____
_____
_____
_____
_____
_____
_____
_____
_____
_____
_____
_____
_____
_____

"O TASTE AND SEE THAT THE LORD IS GOOD."
PSALM 34:8

Eric Richard Williams

CAKE JOURNAL

DAY _____ DATE _____

_____
_____
_____
_____
_____
_____
_____
_____
_____
_____
_____
_____
_____
_____
_____
_____
_____
_____
_____

"O TASTE AND SEE THAT THE LORD IS GOOD."
PSALM 34:8

DIVORCE is a Piece of Cake

CAKE JOURNAL

DAY _____ DATE _____

_____
_____
_____
_____
_____
_____
_____
_____
_____
_____
_____
_____
_____
_____
_____
_____
_____
_____
_____
_____

"O TASTE AND SEE THAT THE LORD IS GOOD."
PSALM 34:8

Eric Richard Williams

CAKE JOURNAL

DAY _____ DATE _____

_____
_____
_____
_____
_____
_____
_____
_____
_____
_____
_____
_____
_____
_____
_____
_____

"O TASTE AND SEE THAT THE LORD IS GOOD."
PSALM 34:8

DIVORCE is a Piece of Cake

CAKE JOURNAL

DAY _____ DATE _____

_____
_____
_____
_____
_____
_____
_____
_____
_____
_____
_____
_____
_____
_____
_____
_____
_____
_____
_____

"O TASTE AND SEE THAT THE LORD IS GOOD."
PSALM 34:8

Eric Richard Williams

CAKE JOURNAL

DAY _____ DATE _____

_____
_____
_____
_____
_____
_____
_____
_____
_____
_____
_____
_____
_____
_____
_____
_____
_____
_____
_____

"O TASTE AND SEE THAT THE LORD IS GOOD."
PSALM 34:8

DIVORCE is a Piece of Cake

CAKE JOURNAL

DAY _____ DATE _____

_____
_____
_____
_____
_____
_____
_____
_____
_____
_____
_____
_____
_____
_____
_____
_____
_____
_____
_____
_____
_____

"O TASTE AND SEE THAT THE LORD IS GOOD."
PSALM 34:8

Eric Richard Williams

CAKE JOURNAL

DAY _____ DATE _____

_____
_____
_____
_____
_____
_____
_____
_____
_____
_____
_____
_____
_____
_____
_____
_____
_____
_____
_____
_____

"O TASTE AND SEE THAT THE LORD IS GOOD."
PSALM 34:8

DIVORCE is a Piece of Cake

CAKE JOURNAL

DAY _____ DATE _____

_____
_____
_____
_____
_____
_____
_____
_____
_____
_____
_____
_____
_____
_____
_____
_____
_____
_____
_____

"O TASTE AND SEE THAT THE LORD IS GOOD."
PSALM 34:8

Eric Richard Williams

CAKE JOURNAL

DAY _____ DATE _____

_____
_____
_____
_____
_____
_____
_____
_____
_____
_____
_____
_____
_____
_____
_____
_____
_____
_____
_____

"O TASTE AND SEE THAT THE LORD IS GOOD."
PSALM 34:8

DIVORCE is a Piece of Cake

CAKE JOURNAL

DAY _____ DATE _____

_____
_____
_____
_____
_____
_____
_____
_____
_____
_____
_____
_____
_____
_____
_____
_____
_____
_____
_____
_____

"O TASTE AND SEE THAT THE LORD IS GOOD."
PSALM 34:8

Eric Richard Williams

CAKE JOURNAL

DAY _____ DATE _____

_____
_____
_____
_____
_____
_____
_____
_____
_____
_____
_____
_____
_____
_____
_____
_____
_____
_____
_____
_____

"O TASTE AND SEE THAT THE LORD IS GOOD."
PSALM 34:8

DIVORCE is a Piece of Cake

CAKE JOURNAL

DAY _____ DATE _____

_____
_____
_____
_____
_____
_____
_____
_____
_____
_____
_____
_____
_____
_____
_____
_____
_____
_____
_____

"O TASTE AND SEE THAT THE LORD IS GOOD."
PSALM 34:8

Eric Richard Williams

CAKE JOURNAL

DAY _____ DATE _____

_____
_____
_____
_____
_____
_____
_____
_____
_____
_____
_____
_____
_____
_____
_____
_____
_____
_____
_____
_____
_____

"O TASTE AND SEE THAT THE LORD IS GOOD."
PSALM 34:8

DIVORCE is a Piece of Cake

CAKE JOURNAL

DAY _____ DATE _____

_____
_____
_____
_____
_____
_____
_____
_____
_____
_____
_____
_____
_____
_____
_____
_____
_____
_____
_____
_____
_____

"O TASTE AND SEE THAT THE LORD IS GOOD."
PSALM 34:8

Eric Richard Williams

CAKE JOURNAL

DAY _____ DATE _____

_____
_____
_____
_____
_____
_____
_____
_____
_____
_____
_____
_____
_____
_____
_____
_____
_____
_____
_____
_____

"O TASTE AND SEE THAT THE LORD IS GOOD."
PSALM 34:8

DIVORCE is a Piece of Cake

CAKE JOURNAL

DAY _____ DATE _____

_____
_____
_____
_____
_____
_____
_____
_____
_____
_____
_____
_____
_____
_____
_____
_____
_____
_____
_____

"O TASTE AND SEE THAT THE LORD IS GOOD."
PSALM 34:8

E-MAIL THE AUTHOR

If this book has **EDUCATED**, **EMPOWERED** and/or **ENCOURAGED** you, please send a letter to Eric Richard Williams at

DIVORCECAKE@cs.com

For Speaking Engagements

Eric Richard Williams
(609) 871-1508 (phone)
(609) 584-1763 (fax)

DIVORCECAKE@cs.com (E-mail)

Made in United States
Troutdale, OR
08/01/2023